More Heat than Light?
Sex-difference Science &
the Study of Language

OTHER BOOKS BY DEBORAH CAMERON

SINGLE-AUTHORED

Feminism and Linguistic Theory, 1992

Verbal Hygiene, 1995; 2012

Good to Talk? Living and Working in a Communication Culture, 2000

Working with Spoken Discourse, 2001

On Language and Sexual Politics, 2006

The Myth of Mars and Venus: Do Men and Women Really Speak Different Languages? 2007

The Teacher's Guide to Grammar, 2007

JOINT-AUTHORED

The Lust to Kill: A Feminist Perspective on Sexual Murder, with Elizabeth Frazer, 1987

Analysing Conversation: Rules and Units in the Structure of Talk, with Talbot Taylor, 1987

Researching Language: Issues of Power and Method, with Elizabeth Frazer, Penelope Harvey, Ben Rampton and Kay Richardson, 1992

The Words Between the Spaces, with Thomas Markus, 2002

Language and Sexuality, with Don Kulick, 2003

EDITED VOLUMES

The Feminist Critique of Language: A Reader, 1990; 1998

Women in their Speech Communities: New Perspectives on Language and Sex, with Jennifer Coates, 1988

Globalization and Language Teaching, with David Block, 2002

The Language and Sexuality Reader, with Don Kulick, 2006

The Trouble & Strife Reader, with Joan Scanlon, 2009

More Heat than Light?
Sex-difference Science & the Study of Language

THE 2012 GARNETT SEDGEWICK MEMORIAL LECTURE

Deborah Cameron

RONSDALE PRESS
VANCOUVER

MORE HEAT THAN LIGHT?
SEX-DIFFERENCE SCIENCE & THE STUDY OF LANGUAGE
Copyright © 2012 Deborah Cameron

Ronsdale Press
3350 West 21st Avenue
Vancouver, B.C., Canada
V6S 1G7

Set in Minion: 11 on 15
Typesetting: Nathan Waddington
Printing: Island Blue, Victoria, B.C., Canada
Cover Design: Nathan Waddington
"Dissent of Woman" © Angela Martin, first published in *Trouble & Strife*
"Own People" © Jacky Fleming, www.jackyfleming.co.uk

Ronsdale Press wishes to thank the following for their support of its publishing program: the Canada Council for the Arts, the Government of Canada through the Canada Book Fund, the British Columbia Arts Council, and the Province of British Columbia through the British Columbia Book Publishing Tax Credit program.

Library and Archives Canada Cataloguing in Publication

Cameron, Deborah, 1958-
      More heat than light: sex-difference science & the study of language / Deborah Cameron.

(Garnett Sedgewick memorial lecture; 2012)
Includes bibliographical references.
Issued also in electronic formats.
ISBN 978-1-55380-221-1

      1. Language and languages--Sex differences. 2. Sociolinguistics.
I. Title. II. Series: Garnett Sedgewick memorial lecture; 2012.

P120.S48C34 2012   306.44   C2012-904851-8

More Heat than Light?
Sex-difference Science & the Study of Language

Garnett Sedgewick, a specialist in Shakespeare, was the first head of the English Department at the University of British Columbia. He served as head from 1920 to 1948. The Sedgewick lectures began in 1955 and honour our first head along with his legacy of literary scholarship at UBC. These lectures are given annually by prominent and accomplished scholars from a variety of areas within English studies and from a variety of locations (and occasionally from UBC itself). Famous Sedgewick lecturers have included Harry Levin, Hugh MacLennan, Northrop Frye, Anne McClintock, Jonathan Goldberg, our own William H. New and Paul Stanwood, and, most recently, Jonathan Gil Harris.

The Sedgewick Lecturer for 2012 is Deborah Cameron, who glories in the title of Rupert Murdoch Professor of Language and Communication at Oxford University. In the context of the Sedgewick Lectures, Dr. Cameron's appearance was especially noteworthy as it marked the first time that the lecture had been given by a linguist. Since the English Department at the University of British Columbia includes linguists as well as literary specialists, I felt that an invitation to a linguist was overdue.

Originally Scottish, Deborah Cameron has established herself as one of the leading sociolinguists of her generation. She is the author of several books and numerous articles and book chapters. Her best-known books are perhaps *Verbal Hygiene* (1995), a book that has been enormously influential and which is soon to be reissued, and, more recently, *The Myth of Mars and Venus: Do Men and Women Really Speak Different Languages?* (2007).

Throughout her career, Professor Cameron has been concerned with the things people know—or think they know—about language usage. In particular, she has been interested and has published with great distinction on the relation of gender and sexuality to language use. It is important to note that this interest is not only academic: Professor Cameron has been and remains an active feminist and has been, as she says, "increasingly involved in communicating with a wider audience about language and linguistic research."

Professor Cameron's Sedgewick Lecture demonstrated all the qualities I have mentioned: it was erudite, wide-ranging and displayed an enviable grasp of a number of technical issues, but it was also clear and accessible. Professor Cameron sketched the history of the belief that men and women use language differently and then went on to argue eloquently, forcefully, and with great panache against this belief. By the end of the lecture, the audience had been entertained and enlightened. Professor Cameron demonstrated that she is equally accomplished in both the theory and the practice of language use.

— Stephen Guy-Bray,
Professor and Head

MORE HEAT THAN LIGHT?
SEX-DIFFERENCE SCIENCE & THE STUDY OF LANGUAGE

My title alludes to the writings of Garnett Sedgewick, the distinguished Canadian scholar for whom these lectures are named. "More heat than light" was the name of the column which he contributed for some years to the *Vancouver Sun* newspaper. I do not know whether Sedgewick ever took up the subject of sex-differences in his column, but I do know there has been debate about his attitudes to women. Some say he was a misogynist, a man who had no regard for women and preferred not to teach them; others dispute that, including some of the women he actually did teach.[1] No one disputes, however, that until very late in his career his policy at the University of British Columbia was to segregate introductory literature classes by gender. That might suggest that he subscribed to, or at least did not dissent from, the belief that, intellectually as well as physically, men and women were different kinds of beings.

Historically, that belief has been commonplace, and often held by men whose views on other kinds of differences among humans posed a challenge to conventional wisdom. The philosopher Jean-Jacques Rousseau, for example, is remembered for his assertion that freedom is every man's birthright; yet in his treatise on education, *Émile*, he made clear that women were not to be treated in the same way as men, since nature had not endowed them with the same powers of reason. Charles Darwin, whose theory of evolution profoundly changed our understanding of what it means to be human, was a believer in racial equality and a passionate opponent of slavery; but he too believed that nature had not made the sexes equal. His major work on human evolution, *The Descent of Man, and Selection by Sex*, contains the following passage:

> The chief distinction in the intellectual powers of the two sexes is shewn by man attaining to a higher eminence, in whatever he takes up, than woman can attain—whether requiring deep thought, reason or imagination, or merely the use of the senses and hands. If two lists were made of the most eminent men and women in poetry, painting, sculpture, music . . . history, science and philosophy . . . the two lists would not bear comparison. . . . If men are capable of decided eminence over women in many subjects the average standard of mental power in man must be above that of woman. . . . It is, indeed, fortunate that the law of the equal transmission of characters to both sexes has commonly prevailed throughout the whole class of mammals; otherwise it is probable that man would have become as superior in mental endowment to woman, as the peacock is in ornamental plumage to the peahen.[2]

Yet Darwin made a far more positive contribution to the feminist thinking of his time than passages like the one just quoted might suggest. Many feminists were attracted to his work because they recognized the profound implications of a theory which said that every species developed through a continuous process of change and adaptation. From that postulate it followed that the inequalities of the past and present might be attenuated or erased in some hypothetical future—a point underlined by the American suffragist Antoinette Brown Blackwell when in 1875 she charged Darwin with failing to follow his own logic where it led. "Mr Darwin," she wrote, "has failed to hold definitely before his mind the principle that the difference of sex, whatever it may consist in, must itself be subject to natural selection and to evolution."[3] To Blackwell, that principle offered a compelling argument for changing the social conditions which had restricted the development of one sex relative to the other, by educating women to the same level as men, and allowing them to participate in a similar range of activities. Noting that the same argument appeared in many other writings by supporters of women's rights in the last decades of the 19th century, the critic Angelique Richardson concludes that "Darwin's

Charles Darwin (1809–1882)

ideas . . . proved valuable to Victorian women writers in countering prohibitive essentialist ideas about sexual difference."[4]

The same observation could not so easily be made about the kinds of Darwinian thinking which have most popular currency and influence today. Far from treating human nature as something always in the process of becoming, contemporary currents, like evolutionary psychology, present it as something set in stone, a matter of the traits we inherit from our earliest human ancestors. These new currents also emphasize that the traits in question are sex-differentiated, just like the social and reproductive roles of early humans. *Ex hypothesi*, it was not advantageous to our male and female ancestors to have the same ways of thinking, feeling and behaving. Males, as hunters and warriors, did best if they were aggressive and competitive; females, as gatherers and nurturers of children, did better if they were co-operative and empathetic. Natural selection ensured that these differences became part of the human genetic blueprint—or in the much-used metaphor of our own time, "hard-wired."

Far from "countering prohibitive essentialist ideas about sexual difference," then, today's version of Darwin rehabilitates essentialist ideas about sexual difference which had previously been out of favour for several decades. Here I want to consider two questions about this development. One is a question about the history of ideas: why has the postulate of hard-wired sexual difference enjoyed such a spectacular resurgence since the 1990s? The other is a question about the science of sex-difference: how far does the evidence support the new essentialism?

Advocates of the new essentialism might well reply that my two questions are actually indivisible: the idea of hard-wired sex differences has returned to favour precisely *because* the evidence supports it. Recent advances in knowledge, especially in genetics and neuroscience, have strengthened the essentialist case while undermining the feminist or social constructionist alternative.[5] I will argue, by contrast, that in at least one key area of inquiry, dealing with sex-differences in verbal ability and behaviour, the new essentialism is not preferable to social constructionist accounts. It is popular for cultural rather than purely scientific reasons. In making that case, and so attempting to shed light on what is currently a very heated debate, I will draw on two intellectual traditions which are well represented in the department Garnett Sedgewick once presided over: on one hand linguistics, and on the other, cultural history.

I have chosen to focus on language for the obvious reason that I am a linguist, and the relationship between language and gender is a subject I can claim to know something about. But that does not mean I am pursuing some minor side-issue which is ultimately peripheral to the new Darwinian account of human nature. On the contrary, language is central to that account, and it is not difficult to see why. The evidence is strong that the human capacity for language is part of our genetic endowment, and thus axiomatically a product of evolution. That much I am not going to question: what I am going to question is what sex has to do with it.

What the new Darwinians think sex has to do with it depends on what general account they favour of how and why language evolved. That remains a contested question. The evolutionary advantages of language might seem obvious, but the human language faculty has significant costs: it requires a very large brain which consumes a lot of fuel and does a lot of its developing after human infants are born, making those infants helpless and dependent for a long period. How do we explain why that was a price worth paying? Or to put it in classic Darwinian terms, how did the ability to speak enhance the fitness of humans, their ability to survive and pass on their genes by reproducing?

One traditional answer to that question suggested that language enhanced survival by enabling humans to co-ordinate joint activities like hunting and warfare. Among early humans it is assumed that those were male activities, so in this story language evolved first among males. But today many scientists subscribe to a competing story, in which the main adaptive function language served was social networking: it allowed members of a species whose survival depends on co-operating in groups to manage their social relationships more efficiently, and to reinforce the bonds that held groups together.[6] In this story it was females who were at the forefront of language evolution. Females tend to be at the centre of most primate social networks, and it is also argued that their role as gatherers and carers gave early human females more time and inclination to engage in social interaction. On this view, the prototypical conversation was not a group of men discussing where the best hunting grounds were, it was a group of women gossiping. But there is also a group of scientists who argue that the prime function for which language evolved was not social networking but courtship.[7] This theory says that speaking among ancestral humans served the same purpose as the peacock's tail: it enabled individual males to display their reproductive fitness, and females to judge which males would make the best mates. Adherents of this view point out that using language to show off is still a largely male preserve. It is men who dominate oral performance genres from political oratory to stand-up comedy and rap.

Clearly, all these stories are speculative. We cannot go back in time to observe our earliest ancestors, and their linguistic behaviour, unlike many other aspects of their lives, has left no archaeological traces for us to study. Before the advent of writing we have no way of knowing what human languages were like, let alone how they were used. So in discussions of the hypothetical scenarios just outlined, it is common for scientists to rely heavily on observations about the linguistic behaviour of modern humans, and particularly on generalizations about the differing behaviour of men and women. Today's male-female language differences are assumed to be expressions of the differing biological traits produced by natural selection many millennia ago. That assumption is itself questionable, as I will explain later on. But even if we accept it for the sake of argument, it is still striking that the scientists emphasize different differences depending on which of the competing evolutionary stories they are using the modern evidence to support. The social network theorists fasten on the continuing stereotypical association of gossip with women, for instance, whereas the courtship theorists draw attention to the equally stereotypical association of oral performance genres with men.

But the issue which looms largest in scientific debates about sex and language evolution—and the one which, as we will see, has the most serious real-world political consequences—is verbal ability, and which sex has been endowed by nature with more of it. Scientific ideas on this subject have shifted dramatically during the

Otto Jespersen (1860–1943)

past century. In 1922, the Danish scholar Otto Jespersen published a book entitled *Language: Its Origins, Nature and Development*, in which he included a chapter on the subject of "The Woman."[8] It was one of the first attempts to summarize what was known about linguistic variation linked to the sex of the speaker. Much of the material Jespersen surveyed was anecdotal rather than scientific, but some of it came from experimental studies conducted by experts in what was then the relatively new discipline of psychology. For instance, Jespersen reports on a study which found that men had more extensive and varied vocabularies than women. He also describes an experiment that set out to determine whether there were sex-differences in reading speed, and found that on average, the women read more quickly than the men. Here is his comment on that result:

> But . . . this rapidity was no proof of intellectual power, and some of the slowest readers were highly distinguished men. . . . With the quick reader it is as though every statement were admitted immediately and without inspection to fill the vacant chambers of the mind, while with the slow reader every statement undergoes an instinctive process of cross-examination.[9]

And here, in stark contrast, is what one respected contemporary authority, the Canadian psychologist Doreen Kimura, had to say on the same subject in 1999:

The impression many people have, that women generally possess better skill with words than men do, probably arises from differences apparent between very young girls and boys. . . . Girls on average articulate earlier and better than boys, and produce longer sentences . . . they also have larger working vocabularies at very young ages. Girls speak more grammatically and . . . are better spellers. . . . Reading is also typically superior in girls. Finally, they are more "fluent" on tests requiring them to generate words with particular limitations on them (such as words containing particular letters), though they are not necessarily more fluent in narrative output.[10]

In the 1920s Jespersen took it for granted that men's verbal abilities were superior to women's; by the end of the century Kimura was equally certain that the opposite was true. What is responsible for this reversal? Put briefly, it reflects a more general shift in assumptions about sex differences in ability. In Jespersen's time, the prevailing view was the one expressed by Darwin in *The Descent of Man*, that women were intellectually inferior to men— or at least, that the most accomplished men would always be superior to even the most exceptional woman. It was also assumed that linguistic abilities were a function of overall intelligence. Hence Jespersen's resort to what from our perspective is an obviously biased interpretation of the reading speed study, that men read more slowly because they think more deeply. Kimura's assertions by contrast reflect the more recent view that there is no significant sex-difference in general intelligence, but more specific abilities do show differences: males on average have better mathematical and spatial skills, while females on average have superior verbal skills.

This more recent orthodoxy has not gone unquestioned. In 1988, Janet Hyde and Marcia Linn published a meta-analysis of studies investigating sex-differences in verbal skill.[11] Meta-analysis is a statistical procedure which aims to discover what the overall trend is in a large collection of research studies of the same question. It involves aggregating the findings from all the studies, using various techniques to make the figures comparable and give more weight to larger or more reliable studies, and then calculating the size of the effect the researchers have collectively found. Effect sizes are conventionally classed as very large, large, moderate, small or close to zero. In the case of the sex and verbal ability, Hyde and Linn found that for most of the verbal abilities which had been tested repeatedly, the overall tendency was for any difference to favour females rather than males—just as someone like Kimura would expect—but the size of the effect was almost always small or close to zero. The clearest exception was spelling accuracy, and even then the effect was only moderate. In 2006, Hyde published a meta-analysis of meta-analyses of sex difference research, in which she examined not only verbal skills but a large range of abilities and traits which have figured repeatedly in studies. For some of these she did find large effects: studies do show, for instance, a substantial difference in how far males and females can throw. But for language her results confirmed what she and Linn had found before: the effect of sex on skill is small or close to zero.[12]

Doreen Kimura (1933–)

As Hyde and Linn commented back in 1988, it is remarkable that a difference so slight should get so much attention. They were mainly talking about the space devoted to it in psychology textbooks, but since they wrote, it has also become a staple in two other kinds of discourse. One is self-help literature; the other is science writing—both academic and popular—about human evolution and what popularizers call "brain sex."

The first of these genres, self-help literature, neither is nor purports to be scientific, and until recently it had no connection with anything you might call hard science. It did, however, have a long-standing concern about the supposed communication gulf between men and women, since this was taken to be at the root of many marital and other relationship problems. In 1990 the linguist Deborah Tannen published a best-selling book, *You Just Don't Understand*, which presented those problems as stemming from systematic differences in the communication styles learned by male and female children in their single-sex peer groups.[13] Two years later, a similar thesis was elaborated by John Gray in a book whose title became one of the most memorable catchphrases of the late 20th century: "men are from Mars, women are from Venus."[14] Women and men are portrayed in this literature as having fundamentally different natures, which find their purest expression in their attitudes to and ways of using language. Where women are gripped by a constant desire to talk, men prefer action to words and often take refuge in silence. When they do talk, men are direct and practical; they do not feel the same need as women to verbalize their thoughts and feelings. In Gray's words:

> Men and women think and process information very differently. Women think out loud, sharing their process of inner discovery with an interested listener. . . . The only times a woman would be silent are when what she had to say would be hurtful. . . . [Women] need to learn that when a man is upset or stressed he will automatically stop talking and go to his "cave" to work things out.[15]

The genre to which these 1990s self-help books belong has been described as "new age psychobabble." Authors presented their thesis using a mixture of anecdotal vignettes featuring invented characters, and observations couched in the language of therapy and "personal growth." They did not claim to have science on their side, and they did not say that the sex-differences they discussed were biologically based. (Tannen explicitly denied that they were; Gray left the question open, offering no explanation beyond a whimsical myth of origin in which women and men came to earth from different planets.) But the 1990s also saw the rise of a new popular science literature inspired by high-profile advances in genetics, evolutionary science and neuroscience. The theme of sex differences was fertile ground for writers in this sub-genre, and there was a spate of books with titles like *Brain Sex, The Female Brain, The Essential Difference* and the *Sexual Paradox*.[16] These texts made far more use of the stylistic trappings of science—technical terms, statistics, references to scientific studies. But they also borrowed heavily (though often without acknowledgement) from the preceding wave of non-scientific Mars and Venus self-help literature. Essentially, they took an already-established body of anecdotal lore about *how* men and women differed, and grafted on to that a new story about *why* they differed—a story that depended less on psychobabble and more on what you might call "neurobabble."

Perhaps the most dramatic case of self-help being rewritten as science is Louann Brizendine's 2006 bestseller *The Female Brain,* which made headlines around the world with its statistical claim that women on average utter 20,000 words in a day, while the male average is a paltry 7,000. When the linguist Mark Liberman investigated the source of these figures, it turned out that they were lifted from a self-help book whose author almost certainly made them up.[17] In 2007 some researchers in Arizona set out to answer the question by doing a real study, which found the average daily word count to be approximately 16,000 words for both sexes.[18] There were large individual differences, but no significant sex-difference at all.

A subtler example is Susan Pinker's 2008 book *The Sexual Paradox,* less popular than *The Female Brain* but more respectfully reviewed, which has this to say about language and sexual difference:

> Male brains are simply less versatile when it comes to language. . . . Much of this versatility has to do with the way the two cerebral hemispheres are organized for language storage and retrieval in men and women. MRI studies show that males have most language functions organized in one hemisphere. Meanwhile, most females use both hemispheres for language. Female brains might be proportionally smaller than male brains, but they are more networked for language.[19]

Pinker cannot be accused of taking her facts from self-help books, but she can be charged with using her scientific sources selectively, and presenting as the unchallenged consensus what is actually a matter of considerable dispute. Four years before *The Sexual Paradox* was published, the journal *Brain* published a meta-analysis of sex and brain lateralization studies, which concluded that overall, MRI studies do not show the difference Pinker says they do.[20] And let us not forget the other meta-analyses mentioned earlier, which question whether there is any significant sex-difference in verbal ability for lateralization studies to explain.

But the books are only the tip of the iceberg. A more serious concern is the increasing influence of neurobabble on professional practice and public policy. The most notable instance is education, where there are currently high-profile campaigns for both the school curriculum and its delivery to be restructured in line with new thinking about brain-sex. Campaigners like Michael Gurian (a well-known advocate of boys' rights) and the US National

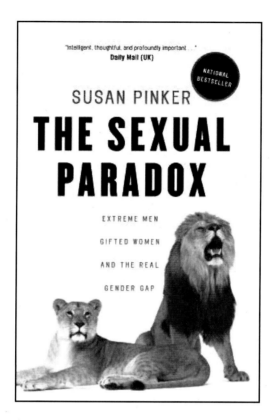

SUSAN PINKER

THE SEXUAL PARADOX

EXTREME MEN

GIFTED WOMEN

AND THE REAL

GENDER GAP

Association for Sex Segregated Public Education (NASSPE) want separate classrooms in which different things will be taught in different ways to boys and girls. Since girls' natural predisposition is to put their every thought into words, teachers should encourage them to share their ideas in talk. Boys, being verbally challenged by nature, need the words uttered in the classroom to be fewer, simpler, louder and accompanied by actions like tossing balls and running relay races. They also need the language element of the curriculum, including foreign languages, literature and even first language literacy, to be kept to the minimum their brain-wiring can handle.

So far there are only a few schools and school districts in the US where these ideas are systematically being put into practice, but the ideas themselves have gained currency and influence because of the way they have been taken up in books and training materials for teachers. The Australia-based psychologist Cordelia Fine reports that she was inspired to write *Delusions of Gender*, a critique of contemporary "neurosexism," when she found her son's class teacher reading a book that claimed boys were biologically incapable of verbalizing their emotions.[21] I have spoken to audiences of college students in the US who had read Michael Gurian's popular manifesto *Boys and Girls Learn Differently!* for an education class[22]—and to audiences in Britain where the teachers present had been on in-service training courses presenting similar claims about sex-differences in learning as incontrovertible scientific facts. These courses, and the associated materials, are typically devised by people who have no training in neuroscience, and are simply reframing what they have read in popular brain-sex literature for an audience of professional educators. Like the popular literature it is based on, the discourse that results over-simplifies and often misrepresents the relevant scientific research.

As an example we might consider a claim made by Dan Hodgins, a popular speaker on the US education conference circuit:

> In females, the corpus callosum is up to 20% larger than in males. . . . Because of this difference in size, females have better verbal abilities and rely heavily on verbal communication; males tend to rely heavily on non-verbal communication and are less likely to verbalize feelings.[23]

The corpus callosum is a structure that links the two hemispheres of the brain; the finding Hodgins alludes to, that it is significantly larger in females, initially sparked interest among scientists but was subsequently queried on the grounds that the researchers had

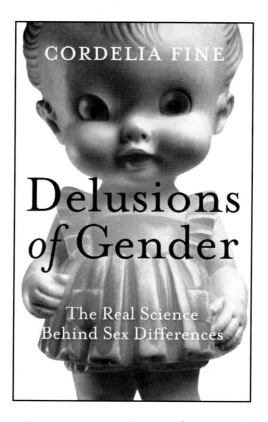

CORDELIA FINE

Delusions
of Gender

The Real Science
Behind Sex Differences

made an error in measurement. In 1997, the journal *Neuroscience and Behavioral Reviews* published an article entitled "Sex differences in the human corpus callosum: myth or reality?" which reviewed the controversy and drew the following conclusion: "The widespread belief that women have a larger splenium [posterior area of the corpus callosum] than men and consequently think differently is untenable."[24] Apparently this did not come to the attention of Dan Hodgins, who was still repeating the opposite point several years after the article appeared. Even if the splenium *were* larger in females, that in itself would not license the conclusion that they think differently: neuroscientists now understand that the relationship between cognitive functioning and the size of the relevant neural structure is considerably more complicated than "bigger means better."

At this point, though, it might reasonably be asked: if I am arguing that the popular literature of brain-sex is pseudo-science, what do I accept as the real thing? Am I suggesting that there are *no* linguistic differences between men and women? Is the intuitive sense almost everyone has, that they do have different ways of communicating verbally, based entirely on prejudice and not at all on substance?

The short answer is no, I am not suggesting there are no gender differences in verbal behaviour. Sociolinguistic research shows that such differences are pervasive. It is hard to think of any study which has looked for them and failed to find any. But what the linguistic research evidence shows is not what evolutionary psychologists and brain-sex writers claim it shows. It does not show, for example, that there are timeless and universal differences between male and female speakers, though that is what you might expect to find if the differences were products of some ancient biological inheritance. Though gender differences themselves do seem to exist in all speech communities, the specific patterns of language-use linked to gender are variable in time and space.

Today, for instance, it is a typical finding, at least in western societies, that women tend to be ahead of men in the adoption and the use of high prestige linguistic variants. Numerous commentators who are not linguists have adduced this as supporting evidence for the superior verbal abilities of females relative to males.[25] But apart from the fact that this reasoning is linguistically naive—what counts as "correct" grammar or pronunciation, and is therefore accorded prestige, is decided by social rather than linguistic criteria, and as such has no connection to verbal ability—we know from the work of historical sociolinguists that the "women speak more 'correctly'" pattern did not prevail in earlier historical periods. In

Tudor and Stuart England (i.e. the 16th and 17th centuries, which must count as the very recent past by the standards of evolutionary science), men were ahead of women in the use of prestigious grammatical forms, a finding which the researchers explain by observing that at the time in question even women of the highest social rank had less education than their male counterparts, far lower rates of literacy and no access to the learned professions.[26] Similarly, in contemporary societies where women continue to be excluded from key domains for the acquisition of prestigious language forms—for instance, in parts of the Arab world where those forms are taught most systematically in religious institutions—you also do not see the typical modern gender pattern.[27]

In sum, both historical and cross-cultural evidence suggest that the gender-linked pattern uncovered by variationist sociolinguistics is not biological, it is social, reflecting not women's or men's innate capacities, but their differential access to and uptake of educational and occupational opportunities. Today's pattern reflects not only western women's equal access to education, but also their not-so-equal position in the labour market: women are still more likely to be channelled into sectors like secretarial and clerical work which require more standard language and literacy skills than the jobs done by men of equivalent status.

Another thing the sociolinguistic evidence shows is the extent of variation *within* gender groups. The linguistic differences among men or among women are usually as great as, and sometimes they are greater than, the average difference between the two groups. This points to something more complicated than the Darwinian story of biologically-based sex-difference, though arguably it has as much to tell us about the nature of human beings. To illustrate what it might tell us, I'd like to take you briefly on a journey to Meiji-era Japan. Japanese is a language that exhibits, at least in its standard form, very marked gender differentiation. The

Japanese female school students dressed in hakama *(the same garment typically worn by male students) in 1877. (Courtesy of Ochanomizu University Library)*

linguist Momoko Nakamura has carried out extensive research on the history of this phenomenon, and I am indebted to her work for this example.[28]

Japanese female school students wearing the kimono *in 1885.*
(Courtesy of Ochanomizu University Library)

In 1879, the Emperor of Japan decreed that girls should in future be educated in their own schools, where they would learn what they needed to know to be good wives and wise mothers. Previously, the few girls who had gone to school at all had attended boys' schools, where they were treated and even dressed exactly like boys. The Emperor's decree thus created a new social category: the schoolgirl. And that in turn created an audience for a new cultural product: the schoolgirl story, which began to appear regularly in newspapers, and soon became popular with young female readers. The authors of this new fictional genre, invariably male, faced an interesting linguistic problem: how to represent the speech of schoolgirls in the dialogue they gave their characters. Real schoolgirls had not existed for long enough to develop a distinctive style of speaking. But the story-writers hit on a device for constructing one. They took a number of particles which were used in Japanese to indicate a frivolous or non-serious stance—items like *teyo* and *dawa*—and added them liberally to the utterances of schoolgirl characters. You could think of these particles as a sort of grammatical giggle: in context, the effect was one of silliness and superficiality. Crucially, however, these qualities were not given to all the characters in schoolgirl stories. The prototypical heroine was a sensible girl who aspired to be a good wife and wise mother, and she did not use the particles at all. They were used most heavily by characters who diverged markedly from the ideal, and whose downfall was dramatized in the narrative.

These conventions did not remain confined to fiction. During the 1880s, disapproving comments began to appear in print on what the commentators labelled "schoolgirl language," meaning the constant use of *teyo* and *dawa* among adolescent females. These features were to late 19th-century Japanese what "like" and high rising intonation contours are to adult English-speakers now—irritating verbal tics associated with silly teenage girls. But in the Japanese case it was life that imitated art: the convention originated in fiction written about schoolgirls by middle-aged men, and was later picked up by the schoolgirls themselves. The intriguing question is why real schoolgirls took their cue from a fictional representation—especially when that representation was overtly negative, stereotyping the girls who used *teyo* and *dawa* as shallow and foolish, while crediting girls who avoided the particles with maturity and moral worth. Nakamura thinks that was probably the point. Then as now, there as here, bad girls are cooler than good girls. Real schoolgirls identified not with the heroines who were held up to them as models, but with the characters who rebelled against the "good wife and wise mother" ideal. They adopted those characters' speech style to mark their own identity—not only as schoolgirls rather than schoolboys, but also and importantly as bad girls rather than good girls.

This example epitomizes many of the key insights that have emerged from recent sociolinguistic research on language and gender. The most important reason why men and women, or boys and girls, talk differently, has nothing to do with innate differences in verbal ability or the preferences we inherit from our early human ancestors. What it has everything to do with is identity, and the way language serves as a symbolic resource for its construction. Language is even better for this purpose than clothing or hair-styles. Tiny nuances of pronunciation, intonation, word-choice or particle-use convey a wealth of information about who the speaker feels she is, or is like, and who she is not, or is different from. Clustering linguistic features together into a culturally recognizable style becomes the outward and audible sign of membership in an imagined community. If many linguistic styles are gendered, that is because gender is a core component of most people's identity. But gender is never identity on its own: it is always inflected by all the other distinctions that make a difference, like social class and ethnicity and generation and subculture. That is why linguists who study the relationship between language and gender do not find it to be monolithic, a question of (all) men (always) talking like this and (all) women (always) talking like that.

Communicating gender is not only about communicating which of the genders you belong to, but what stance you adopt in relation to the different forms of masculinity and femininity your culture makes available.

This way of using language, as a symbolic resource for communicating information about the self and its relation to others, speaks to an aspect of human nature which, if we believe in the idea at all, is as striking as any of the aspects discussed by evolutionary psychologists: the fact that most humans have both a strong desire to be part of a group, and a highly developed consciousness of themselves as individuals. If we take seriously the proposition that our early human ancestors were very like us in their essential natures, then we should surely consider the possibility that even among these small bands of foraging nomads there would have been some variability in communication styles, and some scope for individuals to assert their personalities and their allegiances through speech.

But like everyone else who says anything on this subject, I am speculating; I want to end by reflecting on something that isn't just speculation, namely the resurgent popularity of essentialist discourses on sex-difference. If this is not the result of some Kuhnian scientific revolution in our understanding of human behaviour—and I have argued that it is not, since the popular literature on evolution and brain-sex is actually very unscientific—then how can it be explained?

I would explain it using the same framework I have just used in outlining some of the real reasons why gender-linked linguistic variation is pervasive. In my view, the resurgence of essentialism is fundamentally an imaginative response to the anxieties provoked by recent social changes. The effect of those changes—some brought about by political feminism, others by-products of other socially significant changes, economic and technological—has been to make contemporary men and women, especially educated western ones, less different, and less constrained by their biology, than men and women have ever been before in human history. Educational opportunities, career choices, sexual behaviour and familial or parental roles—even styles of clothing and bodily adornment—are all far less sharply differentiated by gender today than they were 40 or 50 years ago. But since gender remains extremely salient for our understanding of our own and others' identities, the levelling of sharp gender distinctions causes ambivalence and anxiety. What the new essentialism does is reassure people who feel that anxiety that however similar men and women may now appear on the surface, deep down where it really counts, in our minds and in our genes, we are and always will be profoundly different.

. . . . The dissent of woman . . . . . .

I doubt this will have the effect of actually reversing the social and political gains made by women since Darwin's time; but I do think it is an obstacle to dealing with the inequities that still persist, since it encourages an understanding of them as the inevitable and immutable consequences of fundamental differences in men's and women's natures. Liberal neo-Darwinians may concede that some of the changes sought by feminists were desirable on grounds of social justice, but they also suggest that the process of change has now gone as far as it can or should go. That seems to be the position of, for instance, Simon Baron-Cohen, an expert on autism whose influential book *The Essential Difference* argues that female brains evolved to empathize and male ones to "systemize" (i.e., understand the workings of complex systems). It follows that the gender divisions we still observe in the labour market are only the result of people following their natural aptitudes and preferences, and not the consequences of discrimination, historical exclusion or cultural perceptions of what is gender-appropriate. As Baron-Cohen explains:

> People with the female brain make the most wonderful counsellors, primary school teachers, nurses, carers, therapists, social workers, mediators, group facilitators or personnel staff. . . . People with the male brain make the most wonderful scientists, engineers, mechanics, technicians, musicians, architects, electricians, plumbers, taxonomists, catalogists, bankers, toolmakers, programmers or even lawyers.[29]

Feminists have been here before. In 1894, the novelist, feminist and Darwinist Mona Caird mounted a withering attack on the kind of argument which implied, as she put it,

> that the whole race of women has been specially created in order to occupy precisely the position which they occupy at this era, with precisely the amount of freedom now accorded, neither more nor less; for the happy moment has apparently arrived when matters have reached perfection.[30]

Underlining what she saw as the self-evident absurdity of that view, Caird went on:

> We should only laugh at anyone who urged that, for instance, a sailor had been from birth incapable of

understanding a legal document; that had he chosen the barrister's profession instead of his own he would, to the end of his days, have betrayed an ineradicable tendency to run up masts and dance the hornpipe.[31]

"Own People"

What Caird lampooned in 1894, presenting it as a proposition no serious commentator would ever advance, is now advanced in all seriousness by writers such as Simon Baron-Cohen; and far from being laughed at, these apostles of the new essentialism are hailed as cutting-edge scientific thinkers and courageous speakers of politically inconvenient truths. In this lecture, however, I have argued that they are neither of those things. Using their arguments about language as my case-study, I have suggested that their science is flawed, and that its popular appeal can be attributed to two main factors, both of them cultural: one is the pervasive anxiety about social change that I mentioned above, while the other is the enormous prestige accorded to knowledge that is or purports to be "scientific."

The cultural prestige of science is even greater today than it was in Darwin's time. But now as in the past, it is my own belief that the study of language, literature and culture has an equally important contribution to make to the perennial debate on what it means to be human. And with that, if with nothing else I have said, I suspect Garnett Sedgewick would have agreed.

1. The subject of Sedgewick's attitudes to women is discussed in Margery Fee, "Puck's green England and the Professor of English," *University of Toronto Quarterly* 64(3): 398–416, 1995. I am indebted to Laurel Brinton for directing me to this source, and for other background information on Sedgewick and UBC.

2. Charles Darwin, *Evolutionary Writings*, ed. J. Secord (Oxford: Oxford University Press, 2008), p. 304.

3. Antoinette Brown Blackwell, *The Sexes Throughout Nature* (New York: Putnam, 1875), p. 16.

4. Angelique Richardson, "Against finality: Darwin, Mill and the end of essentialism," *Critical Quarterly* 53: 21–43, 2011, p. 38. Richardson also presents evidence from both his notebooks and his published writings that Darwin himself took the feminist argument seriously.

5. See e.g. Steven Pinker, *The Blank Slate: The Modern Denial of Human Nature* (London: Allen Lane, 2002).

6. See Robin Dunbar, *Gossip, Grooming and the Evolution of Language* (London: Faber, 1996).

7. See e.g. Geoffrey Miller, "Sexual selection for cultural display," in R. Dunbar, C. Knight and C. Power (eds.) *The Evolution of Culture* (Edinburgh: Edinburgh University Press, 1999); John Locke, *Duels and Duets: Why Men and Women Talk So Differently* (Cambridge: Cambridge University Press, 2011).

8. Otto Jespersen, "The Woman," rep. in Deborah Cameron

(ed.) *The Feminist Critique of Language* (London: Routledge, 1998).

9. Jespersen, "The Woman," p. 239. Jespersen attributes the explanation to [Havelock] Ellis, writing in 1904, but he clearly endorses it himself.

10. Doreen Kimura, *Sex and Cognition* (Cambridge, Mass: MIT Press, 1999), p. 91.

11. Janet S. Hyde and Marcia Linn, "Gender differences in verbal ability: a meta-analysis," *Psychological Bulletin* 104: 53–69, 1988.

12. Janet S. Hyde, "The gender similarities hypothesis," *American Psychologist* 60(6): 581–92, 2005.

13. Deborah Tannen, *You Just Don't Understand: Men and Women in Conversation* (New York: Morrow, 1990).

14. John Gray, *Men are from Mars, Women are from Venus* (New York: HarperCollins, 1992).

15. Ibid., pp.67–69.

16. Anne Moir and David Jessel, *Brain Sex: The Real Difference between Men and Women* (New York: Delta Books, 1991); Louann Brizendine, *The Female Brain* (New York: Morgan Road, 2006); Simon Baron-Cohen, *The Essential Difference: Men, Women and the Extreme Male Brain* (London: Allen Lane, 2003); Susan Pinker, *The Sexual Paradox: Troubled Boys, Gifted Girls and the Real Difference Between the Sexes* (London: Atlantic Books, 2008).

17. See Mark Liberman, "Sex on the brain," *Boston Globe*, 24 September 2006.

18. M. R. Mehl, S. Vazire, N. Ramírez-Esparza, R.B. Slatcher and J.W. Pennebaker, "Are women really more talkative than men?" *Science*, July 6: 82, 2007.

19. Pinker, *The Sexual Paradox*, p. 46.

20. I. Sommer, A. Aleman, A. Bouma & R. Kahn, "Do women

really have more bilateral language representation than men? A meta-analysis of functional imaging studies." *Brain* 127: 1845–52, 2004.

21. Cordelia Fine, *Delusions of Gender: The Real Science Behind Sex Differences* (London: Icon Books, 2010).

22. Michael Gurian and Patricia Henley, with Terry Trueman, *Boys and Girls Learn Differently!* (San Francisco: Jossey-Bass, 2001).

23. Dan Hodgins, "Male-female differences," http://languagelog. ldc.upenn.edu/myl/llog/Hodgins1.pdf., accessed May 1, 2012. I cite this version, made available via the linguistics blog Language Log (which has devoted several posts to debunking Hodgins's claims about brain-sex and learning) because it probably offers the most reliable access for scholars; I first came upon the text from links in other online sources, including NASSPE's website, but these have proved to be more ephemeral. The version cited here carries no date, but other sources suggested to me that the text is a version or transcript of a lecture dating from 2003.

24. K. Bishop and D. Waldsten, "Sex differences in the human corpus callosum: myth or reality?" *Neuroscience and Biobehavioral Reviews* 21(5): 581–601, 1997.

25. Sources in which this equation is made by non-linguists include Baron-Cohen, *The Essential Difference*, Dunbar, *Gossip*, and *Kimura, Sex and Cognition*.

26. See Terttu Nevalainen and Helena Raumolin-Brunberg, *Historical Sociolinguistics* (London: Longman Pearson, 2003).

27. See e.g. Fatima Sadiqui, *Women, Gender and Language in Morocco* (Leiden: Brill, 2003).

28. Momoko Nakamura, "Creating indexicality: schoolgirl speech in Meiji Japan," in Deborah Cameron and Don Kulick (eds.), The *Language and Sexuality Reader* (Milton Park:

Routledge, 2006).

29. Baron-Cohen, *The Essential Difference*, p. 185.

30. Mona Caird, "Suppression of variant types," 1894, repr. in Ann Heilmann (ed.) *The Late Victorian Marriage Question: A Collection of Key New Woman Texts*, Vol. 1. (London: Routledge, 1998), p. 206.

31. Caird, "Suppression of variant types," p. 207.

Deborah Cameron is Professor of Language and Communication in the English Faculty of Oxford University. She was educated in Britain at the universities of Newcastle-upon-Tyne and Oxford; before taking up her present job she taught at several UK universities, and has also held visiting positions in Australia, Sweden and the US. Her research interests include language ideologies, language, gender and sexuality, and the sociolinguistics of globalization. As well as publishing extensively on these topics, she is the author of a textbook on spoken discourse analysis and co-author of a book about linguistic research methods. She regularly writes and broadcasts on linguistic topics for a general audience, and is a longstanding contributor to the British radical feminist magazine *Trouble & Strife*. Her work has been translated into Japanese, Finnish and German.